THE BIG WIND-UP!

...the final book of Nasty 90s cartoons by **AISLIN**

Introduction by Pamela Wallin

Text by Terry Mosher
Book design and colorization by Mary Hughson

McArthur & Company
Toronto

Other books by Aislin:
  Aislin–100 Caricatures (1971)
  Hockey Night in Moscow (1972, with Jack Ludwig)
  Aislin–150 Caricatures (1973)
  The Great Hockey Thaw (1974, with Jack Ludwig)
  'Ello, Morgentaler? Aislin–150 Caricatures (1975)
  O.K. Everybody Take a Valium! Aislin–150 Caricatures (1977)
  L'Humour d'Aislin (1977)
  The Retarded Giant (1977, with Bill Mann)
  The Hecklers: A History of Canadian Political Cartooning (1979, with Peter Desbarats)
  The Year The Expos Almost Won the Pennant (1979, with Brodie Snyder)
  Did the Earth Move? Aislin–180 Caricatures (1980)
  The Year The Expos Finally Won Something (1981, with Brodie Snyder)
  The First Great Canadian Trivia Quiz (1981, with Brodie Snyder)
  Stretchmarks (1982)
  The Anglo Guide to Survival in Quebec (1983, with various Montreal writers)
  Tootle: A Children's Story (1984, with Johan Sarrazin)
  Where's the Trough? (1985)
  Old Whores (1987)
  What's the Big Deal? Questions and Answers on Free Trade (1988, with Rick Salutin)
  The Lawn Jockey (1989)
  Parcel of Rogues (1990, with Maude Barlow)
  Barbed Lyres, Canadian Venomous Verse (1990, with Margaret Atwood and other poets)
  Drawing Bones–15 Years of Cartooning Brian Mulroney (1991)
  Put Up & Shut Up! The '90s so far in Cartoons (1994)
  Oh, Canadians! Hysterically Historical Rhymes (1996, with Gordon Snell)
  One Oar in the Water. The Nasty '90s continued in cartoon (1997)
  Oh, No! More Canadians! Hysterically Historical Rhymes (1998, with Gordon Snell)
  Nick, A Montreal Life (1998, with various writers)
  2000 Reasons to Hate The Millennium (1999, edited by Terry Mosher and Josh Freed)

Canadian Cataloguing in Publication Data

Aislin
  The Big Wind-up!: the last volume of nasty '90s cartoons

ISBN 1-55278-089-9

1. Canada – Politics and government – 1993 –   – Caricatures and cartoons.*
2. Canada – Politics and government – 1984-1993 – Caricatures and cartoons.*
3. Quebec (Province) – Politics and government – 1985-1994 – Caricatures and cartoons.*
4. Quebec (Province) – Politics and government – 1994 –   – Caricatures and cartoons.*
5. Canadian wit and humour, Pictoral.
I. TITLE.

NC1449 A37A4 1999   971.064'7'0207   C99-931745–8

CONTENTS

INTRODUCTION

Each of Aislin's cartoons is a Trojan Horse of ideas and insights – unleashing new thoughts and old outrages in your head.

He is prescient, indignant, funny and oh so on target. In fact most of his cartoons should be registered. They are lethal weapons!

Whether he has in his sights a President, a Prime Minister, a policy or a personality – his aim is true.

It has often been said that it is the journalist who writes the first rough draft of history. And what the political cartoonist does is give us what the news can't and history is supposed to – perspective.

These cartoons are not illustrations for the newspages. Nor are they the work of a stand-up comic or a gadfly. They are dispatches from the front lines of life. And as any good cartoon must be, the "gold standard for generating action."

Aislin, a.k.a. Terry Mosher, makes us think, and provokes the outrage that we should feel and often don't. So we thank him for breaking through the din of the information overload, the cynicism and the torrent of opinionizing that dominates our media-saturated world, to offer some rare moments of joy and of tears!

Pamela Wallin
Toronto
July, 1999

*Special thanks to Gaëtan Côté, Pat Duggan and
the rest of the library staff at The Gazette,
Johanne Norchet, "Toes" Leduc, Kim McArthur
and her gang of wonderful maniacs,
and Mary Hughson (as always).*

JEAN CHRÉTIEN and the CANADIANS

MR. SUHARTO ALWAYS LIKES A LITTLE BIT ON THE SIDE OF HIS PLATE

The pepper spray affair.

"It makes no difference who you vote for – the two parties are really one party representing four percent of the people."
Gore Vidal

Canadians have certainly discovered Vidal's axiom to be true, what with the governing Liberals under Jean Chrétien having absconded with Tory policies during their second term. Despite a series of scandals and Chrétien's constant gaffes – no Einstein, he – the Liberals continue to enjoy an unprecedented run of popularity.

Granted, the economy is soaring, thanks primarily to the Americans. Canadians, too, are interested in political stability after experiencing Brian Mulroney's years of having held conservatives of different stripes together with smoke and mirrors.

The Liberals remain the only truly national party and should continue their current cake-walk well into the new Millennium until some group is capable of merging the squabbling dissident conservative forces against them.

In the meantime, the NDP, the Bloc and the Senate huff and puff along, continuing to supply us with comic relief.

Jean Chrétien visits Russia to discuss business with Boris Yeltsin.

Chrétien caught on a skiing holiday instead of attending the funeral of King Hussein of Jordan.

UNDERCOVER...

Did the RCMP receive direct orders from the PMO leading to the pepper spray affair?

Short-lived cabinet minister Andy Scott, overheard gossiping about confidential matters on an airline flight.

Hepatitis C scandal emerges.

Paul Martin suprises everyone by saying no to the bank mergers.

ERSTWHILE LIBERAL-STAR-ON-THE-HORIZON, ALLAN ROCK LOOKS TO BE IN DEFINITE NEED OF A BLOOD TRANSFUSION

Allan Rock in hot water over Hepatitis C scandal.

The Red Cross is found guilty in the tainted blood scandal.

Conrad Black sues Jean Chrétien for supposedly blocking the newspaper baron's appointment as an English Lord.

The Tory leadership fight goes on at the same time as the release of the animated film, Small Soldiers.

Joe Clark's less than triumphant return as Tory leader.

Launch of a new conservative newspaper, The National Post.

Much talk of the Tories and Reform joining to form the United Alternative.

After a luke-warm reception, talk begins about a possible alternative to the United Alternative.

After Gilles Duceppe wore a shower cap on his head, the condom becomes the unofficial symbol of the Bloc...

We'll stay even if PQ loses: Bloc MPs

Canadian Press

QUEBEC – The Bloc Québécois will probably stick around even if the Parti Québécois loses the next provincial election, MPs from the party say.

Several Bloc MPs questioned by Quebec Le Soleil said the party could stay in Parliament until the PQ is re-elected and another sovereignty referendum is held.

They said they would continue to defend Quebec's interests and promote sovereignty.

It is believed to be the first time Bloc MPs have publicly said they would stay in Ottawa if the PQ lost the election.

"Our main goal is promoting a[nd] achieving sovereignty," Bloc whip Stéphane Bergeron told Le Soleil. "But the temporary objective is still defending Quebec's interests.

"Regardless of the government in Quebec City, these two objectives will remain a priority, and the Bloc's presence in Ottawa will remain perti[n]ent."

Heh, heh...

GOVERNMENT of CANADA
Pension cheque — $$$$$$
M. Capote — Bloc M.P.

...amongst cartoonists, anyway.

29

Meanwhile, on the left...

...Svend Robinson presents a petition to Parliament to drop God from the Constitution.

Perky senators demand free parking at airport

JACK AUBRY
Ottawa Citizen

OTTAWA – Now that they've given themselves a $9,000-a-year housing allowance, senators have set their sights on free parking at Canada's largest airport.

Their noses clearly out of joint, a Senate committee has written to the Toronto airport authority that runs Pearson Airport to complain about the loss of their long-standing parking passes.

Adding to the insult, the senators point out, is that Toronto-area MPs get to keep their free parking. The senators say they, too, are members of Parliament.

The Senate's internal economy committee is the same committee that snuck in, on the last day of the spring session, a new $181-a-day tax-free bonus for senators who actually show up in Ottawa. With the new housing-allowance perk, senators have pushed their remuneration – $64,400 salary and $19,100 in tax-free allowances – to an amount equivalent to a taxable salary of more than $100,000 a year.

When asked whether the airport had taken away his free parking, Senator William Kelly responded: "The rascals have! We have so few perks. We are losing another one."

He said that, whether "you like it or not," senators are also MPs.

Steve Shaw, the vice-president of strategic planning at the airport, says only "elected" MPs will continue to enjoy free parking. A review of parking passes by the authority could only "justify" giving free parking to MPs and not the appointed senators, he said.

Shaw points out that senators are reimbursed for parking fees, so there is no lost revenue for the upper-house members.

Shaw said the 24 Ontario senators, who are appointed by the prime minister, may want to keep their free passes for the prestige or convenience.

"Senators, of course, while they may live here, represent interests all over the place. It's hard to locate them ... we have had to sort of clamp down a bit," said Shaw.

Last fall, for instance, Senator Trevor Eyton said he was claiming so-called senator "public business" days to account for his absences from the Senate to attend such events as SkyDome board meetings or international chamber of commerce meetings in Paris.

Senator Pierre-Claude Nolin, the co-chairman of the internal economy committee, which sent steaming letters to the airport, says no distinction should be made between elected and appointed members of Parliament.

"We expect the airport to reconsider their position. It's not a priority or anything but we are pursuing it," he said.

The authority cut down the number of free parking passes from more than 100 to about 60 at the end of March. Toronto Mayor Mel Lastman and three other area mayors also enjoy the free passes, along with the elected MPs and some airport personnel.

Shaw said the number was cut to increase revenues.

"It's a fairly general policy, given the sort of pressure on parking at the airport. And we have to be thoughtful that it is part of our revenues," explained Shaw.

There was no intent to insult the senators, according to the vice-president.

"Well, senators have reminded us very strongly that they, too, are members of Parliament and should enjoy the same privileges as an elected member of Parliament," he said.

"We are in the process of reviewing that policy. It wasn't intended in any way of getting anyone upset."

He said the authority will decide in the next few weeks how to handle the angry senators.

A BETTER IDEA...

ABOLISHED

AISLIN 98
MONTREAL GAZETTE

Canada to acquire new helicopters.

Canada Post on strike.

Frank Magazine's Glen McGregor is hired by The Citizen.

Air Canada pilots on strike.

The strange demise of Groundhog's Day mascot, Wiarton Willie, inspires a comparison to the fate of the Social Union.

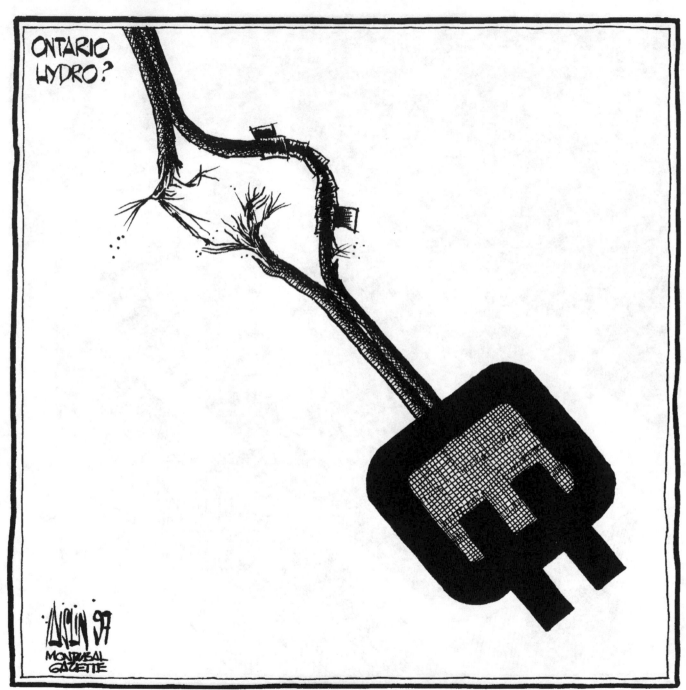

Report indicates that Ontario's nuclear reactors are in trouble.

Ontario Premier Mike Harris is re-elected.

TORONTONIANS ARE NOW THE WORST DRIVERS IN CANADA

Demonstrators upset Ontario electioneering

ONTARIO OFFICIALS FEAR CHAOS AT POLLS

TORONTO MAYOR GOES APES***

Leafs reach Stanley Cup semi-finals!

WHEN EXACTLY DID ONTARIO SUDDENLY BECOME MORE INTERESTING THAN QUEBEC?

AISLIN 99
MONTREAL GAZETTE

Chaos at Canadian airports during bad weather.

Lloyd Axworthy wins kudos for his part in establishing an international treaty on the elimination of land mines.

Much discussion within the Bloc Québécois about whom is a real Quebecker.

Lucien Bouchard keeps mum while visiting China.

LUCIEN BOUCHARD et les QUÉBÉCOIS

WHAT IS THIS?

☐ SOME KNOB WITH A CONDOM ON HIS HEAD AND HIS FOOT IN HIS MOUTH?

☐ A QUEBEC SEPARATIST ASSUMING THIS WEEK'S STANCE ON SOMETHING OR OTHER?

AISLIN '99
MONTREAL GAZETTE

After almost winning Quebec's 1995 referendum, Lucien Bouchard was then anointed as the new Premier, replacing Jacques Parizeau. For a period of time, Bouchard seemed almost invincible.

However, the business of dealing with the day-to-day realities of Canada's most complicated province began to wear away at Bouchard's image.

Meanwhile, just as Bouchard had done earlier, Jean Charest returned from Ottawa to enter the Quebec political arena, becoming the leader of the Liberal Party. Bouchard immediately called a snap election in the fall of 1998, perhaps hoping to take advantage of Charest's newness at the Quebec game.

Running under the campaign slogan *J'ai confiance*, the PQ did win the election with a majority of seats, but only because of Quebec's odd makeup in terms of voter distribution. In actual fact, Charest garnered a higher percentage of the popular vote (43% to 42%).

As we approach the millennium, and another promised referendum, Bouchard's chances of regaining past glories seem shaky at best.

All the while, Jean Charest is patiently waiting for his turn.

Quebec names an official bug.

Lucien Bouchard favours Arrowroot cookies.

Bouchard angered about something or other.

Bouchard attempts to be all things to all people..

Bouchard visits the U.S. to calm the waters.

Quebec finance minister, Bernard Landry.

Jacques Parizeau just can't keep his mouth shut.

MEDIA NEWS IN BRIEF

National Geographic magazine recently published a gloomy article on the subject of life in present-day Quebec.

CBS's news program, 60 Minutes, plans to air a highly critical documentary on the subject of Quebec's Bill 101.

The Parti Québécois is presently seeking a bilingual PR firm.

The PQ suffers from a bad image abroad.

Quebec labour leader, Lorraine Pagé, is found guilty of stealing gloves from The Bay.

Liberals and the PQ are united in their stand against Chretien's idea of a Social Union.

FACT: IF HE WERE TO SAY "NO" NOW, HE'D BE TOAST...

As leader of the federal Tories, Jean Charest had no choice but to return to Quebec and lead the provincial Liberals.

Charest finds the election hard going.

Quebec's nationalist press fail to find fault with PQ.

Doctors in Bouchard's riding bought off during campaign.

Send-up on PQ "J'ai Confiance" campaign

The Quebec election begins to resemble Montreal's notorious biker wars.

Bouchard wins the election. Now, will there be the promised third referendum?

Maclean's Quebec election cover.

Jean Charest as Barney.

Announcing KINKY SPICE!

News Item: One of the Spice Girls quits. Are they looking for a replacement?

Illustration for Willaim Weintraub's play, "The Underdogs".

LOUISE AND THE ANGLOS

ACTUALLY, I SHOP AT OGILVY'S...

In 1998, the American TV program *60 Minutes* filmed a documentary on the Quebec situation, following a language cop through the streets of west-end Montreal. Always conscious of their image abroad, many Francophones were shocked at how buffoon-like Quebec appeared to outsiders in its application of Bill 101.

And, indeed, therein lies the problem. Many Anglophones now understand, if grudgingly, that Bill 101 is meant to guarantee the survival of the French language in Quebec. However, they are often appalled at the insensitivity and stupidity shown in carrying out the law.

Louise Beaudoin, the Quebec minister in charge of language, was interviewed on the same program and came across as arrogant and officious, fitting the many caricatures of her as a whip-wielding

A sketch for Global Television on Quebec election night.

63

The OLF came up with a list of new terms to be used while playing golf. The Gazette refused to publish this cartoon.

Québéculture vs. Canculture.

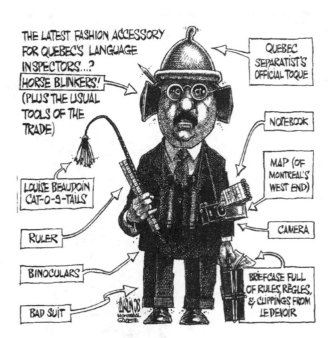

dominatrix. Note, too, that domination has always been thought of as a classic "English" sexual fantasy.

No community in Canada has gone through as dramatic a change as has Quebec's Anglo population over the last thirty years.

However, to think it speaks in one collective voice would be a mistake.

For the time being, the Anglos appear to be far more troubled than they really are, primarily because of a current crop of rigid, and extremely vocal, spokespersons.

The OLF vows to return to Shawville after being ridden out of town on a rail.

Louise's reaction to the possibility of Eaton(s) going back to bilingual signs.

Is Timothy Eaton rolling in his grave these days?

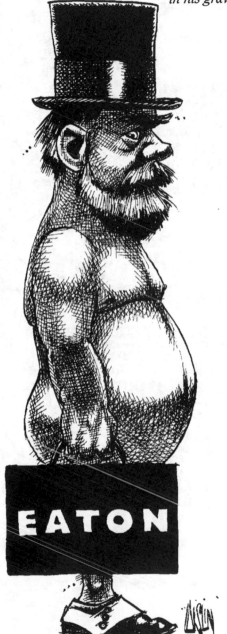

As if Eaton's didn't have problems enough.

Traditional old Montreal clubs try to keep up with the times.

Journalist William Johnson became head of the anglo lobby group Alliance Quebec in 1998.

Subsequently, Johnson attracted many partitionists and other frustrated Anglos to the cause, leading to a mass resignation of almost half of Alli-Q's more compliant board of directors.

But even Johnson wasn't radical enough for the true "angryphones", who found their voice on the airwaves in firebrand radio show host, Howard Galganov. Because of his habit of referring to all separatists as "bastards" and the Quebec fleur-de-lys flag as a "swastika", most Anglos find Galganov to be an extreme embarrassment.

Despite these characters, the traditional French-English animosity is now fading rapidly in Quebec, with younger people no longer possessing any of the traditional old resentments. One just has to look at current graduating classes coming out of McGill University to understand where Montreal is heading.

There is hope regarding the new Anglos (the 20- and 30- somethings), who are generally bilingual, often trilingual, and are all comfortable with each other.

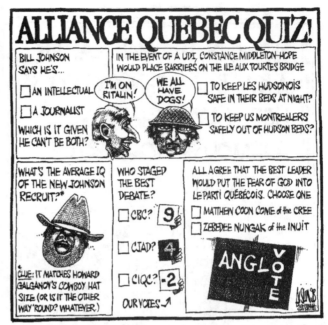

Alliance–Quebec election turns fiery.

Anglo feudings.

More Anglo feudings.

73

Westmount decides to have a SSJB Day party.

"It was clear on Auf der Maur's departure, that he – and his attitude, and his friends – represented Montreal's best hope of coming together as a complex society, instead of falling apart as a series of disjointed ghettos."
From Benoît Aubin's tribute in the book, Nick, A Montreal Life.

A man who signified conciliation in Montreal's Anglo community well before its time was Nick Auf der Maur. As a boulevardier, columnist, politician, and raconteur, Nick moved comfortably in Montreal's downtown circles.

However, Auf der Maur's excessive life-style caught up with him and – a pity – it struck him down in 1998 at the age of 55.

Nick held out hope for all the 3,000 people of all political stripes who attended his funeral at St. Patrick's Cathedral. Some mourners sported Donald Duck ties given Nick's love of the Disney character.

Friends asked that a street be named after Nick and, within a year, an alley off Crescent Street was chosen, a narrow passage that Nick often used to take as a short-cut between bars.

And then, there was the death of another great Montrealer, Jean Drapeau.

A cartoon of Nick Auf der Maur and Tim Burke, after they quit The Gazette to join the renegade Daily News.

Jean Drapeau dies.

Talk of creating a permanent Quebec ID card.

Toronto's weather problems seem tame in comparison to what Montreal suffered during the Ice Storm.

February in Montreal.

Montreal's Grand Prix auto race begs a comparison to Pierre Bourque's running of City Hall.

PIERRE BOURQUE, MONTRÉAL AND THE WEATHER.

Montreal skyline.

Pierre Bourque was elected as the mayor of Montreal in 1994, replacing the tired Jean Doré. A horticulturalist by trade, Bourque promised to reinvigorate Montreal's sluggish economy.

This has happened to a certain extent, but probably has a lot more to do with the spillover from the burgeoning North American market (plus the low Canadian dollar) than with any of Bourque's efforts.

Scandal-ridden, Bourque's Vision party began to disintegrate by the end of his first term as mayor, with a large number of its members either joining other parties or sitting on City Council as independents.

But then, an odd thing happened on Pierre Bourque's way to oblivion in the form of the two individuals who chose to run against him for mayor in 1998.

Jean Doré attempted a comeback. However, Montrealers couldn't forget the man's arrogance during his time as mayor, never mind the memory of the $300,000 window he had had installed in his office at City Hall. Doré managed only a bare 10% of the vote, coming in third.

Jacques Duchesneau had been an extremely popular chief of police. However, when he picked up the mantle and decided to run for mayor, his campaign foundered. He couldn't quite shake the policeman image and was probably hurt by his strong

Montreal's profitable Casino now open 24 hours a day.

public stance in favour of federalism. Montrealer's like their municipal politicians to be neutral on the QuébéCan front.

Therefore, after being written off by virtually everyone, Pierre Bourque was re-elected by default.

He will be helped in his second term by being able to point at Montreal's newfound vigor on the financial front. However, his hands will continue to be tied because of the strong influence now held over Montreal's city council by the governing P.Q. in Quebec City.

Former police chief Jacques Duchesneau runs for mayor...

...while former mayor Jean Doré attempts a comeback.

OUR MAYOR'S CREDIBILITY GAP...

AISLIN 97
MONTREAL GAZETTE

$125,000,000.00

Pierre Bourque (who is rumoured to wear a wig) brings in a budget with a shortfall of a mere $125 million.

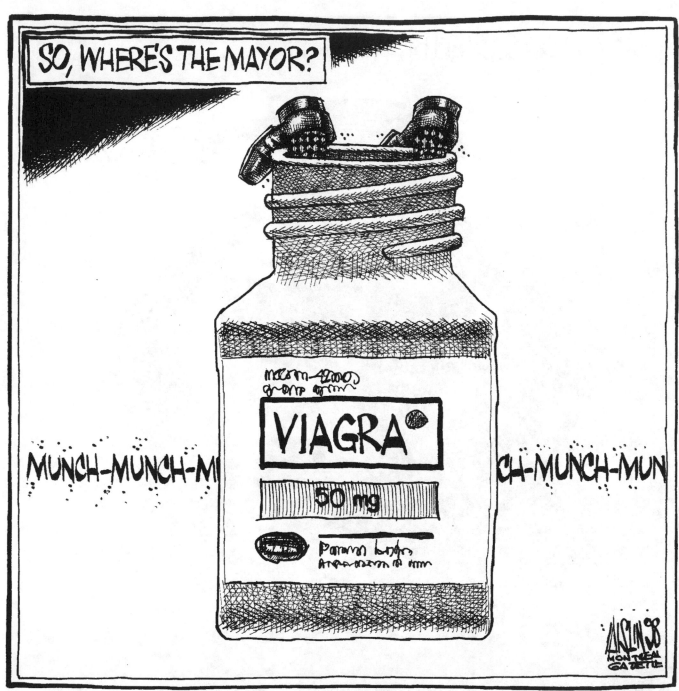

Pierre Bourque starts campaigning hard...

...and, astonishingly, is re-elected.

Our theory: The mayor was totally pixelated when he came up with this one...

Bourque proposes changing English street names in the high-tech sector of city to computer-related names.

To draw attention to their grievances, Montreal's firemen destroy their own equipment.

When the movie Titanic was released on the 1st of January, 1998, all seemed calm in Montreal, until the Ice Storm hit.

Perhaps no other major city in North America is governed so much by the weather as is Montreal. It is a town of extremes and variables, the temperature included, and most of the city's activities – social and otherwise – are determined and measured by the cycle of the weather forecaster.

Of course, Montrealers take some pride in being able to handle these extremes, and never more so than during the infamous ice storm in January of 1998.

This cartoonist must admit to having missed the ice storm completely – being on holiday in the Caribbean. Thus, I felt quite guilty about having missed the storm of the century (even if unintentionally). Ergo, witness the rather sheepish cartoon on the following page.

In contrast to the severe temperatures of January and February, most agree that June and July are probably Montreal's best months, particularly with millions of people wandering the streets during the concurrent Jazz and Comedy Festivals.

And Montreal is also one of North America's safest cities as, despite the festive atmosphere during these various festivals, the police rarely report any major disturbances.

VIEUX MONTRÉAL - Two women dig out their car after the ice storm of January, 1998

Following, you will find a selection of cartoons dealing with one or another of the key events associated with each month of the year in Montreal.

This is followed by a Jazz Festival sketchbook.

AFTER A TWO-WEEK CARIBBEAN HOLIDAY, HERE ARE A FEW GUILTY OBSERVATIONS AFTER HAVING MISSED THE STORM OF THE CENTURY

2 DAYS? THAT'S NOTHIN'! WE WERE OUT FOR 6 DAYS!

6 DAYS? LUXURY LIVING! TRY 9 DAYS!

ONLY 9 DAYS? CHICKEN-FEED!

HEY! LET'S USE THAT GUY WITH THE TAN FOR KINDLING!

OR THIS GREETING FROM PEGGY CURRAN →

IF AISLIN EVEN TRIES TO CARTOON OUR ICE STORM, WE'LL TAR & FEATHER HIM AND SEND HIM TO THE SOUTH SHORE!

BUT, HEY, HASN'T THE LANDSCAPE CHANGED?

CJAD

AND A TIP OF THE HAT TO THE TROOPS FOR DOING WHAT THE BRASS COULDN'T —RESTORING THE ARMY'S GOOD NAME

AISLIN 98
MONTREAL GAZETTE

In January, what is there to look forward to but February.

February is RRSP month.

March means the anticipation of the golf season.

These days, April means the Habs are out of playoffs.

May is planting month.

June, and the shad flies emerge.

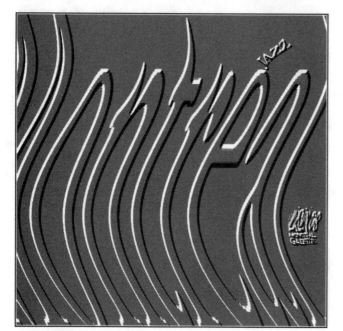

July is Jazz.

Even in August, it can still be hot.

September, and the politics are back in full force.

October foilage.

November brings the first snow.

December's bills.

Most agree, July in Montreal is the best month of all.

AISLIN at the JAZZ FEST

RAY BONNEVILLE CLOWNS AROUND DURING A RAIN DELAY...

THE BLUES AIN'T NOTHIN' BUT A BUNCH OF BEERS!

TOOTS THIELEMANS MICHEL DONATO AT THE OLYMPIA...

THERE ARE MEN IN MONTREAL WHO WOULD GIVE UP ALMOST ANYTHING JUST TO WATCH THE LADY SING "POPSICLE TOES"...

WELL, COULD I GET SOMETHING FRONT AND CENTRE FOR DIANA KRALL IF I TRADED IN MY HABS' SEASON'S TICKETS?

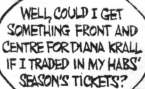

BALCONY—THÉÂTRE ST. DENIS...

WHERE WAS THE PLACE TO BE SEEN THIS YEAR?

THE BRANFORD MARSALIS CONCERT

AND THE PLACE NOT TO BE CAUGHT DEAD?

THE NATIONAL POST COCKTAIL PARTY AT PLANET HOLLYWOOD

JOY! THE PIN STRIPE BAND

YUP, I'M IN BED, SICK AS A DOG, DOCTOR'S ORDERS HAK! HAK! COUGH! BUT, I MIGHT BE BACK AT WORK NEXT WEEK

...THEN DIZ LOOKED AT MY NOSE AND SAID, "MAN, LET ME SEE YOU BLOW THAT THING!"

In June, instead of politics, it was the World Cup, basketball playoffs and hockey finals and...

...the Grand Prix.

Municipal elections? Who cares, they're all the same! In Montreal, it should be that...

Felipe Alou is one of the most popular Montrealers.

FELIPE ALOU AND OTHER SPORTERS

Pan-Am Games goaltender fails urine test, losing Canada the gold medal.

Felipe Alou, the manager of the Montreal Expos, has proved to be one of the most charismatic men in town, even if the baseball team's future is in question. As of this book's printing, the Expos are on the cusp of a new beginning. The team will either be ensconced in a brand new downtown ball park – or disappear from the city entirely.

Interestingly, the roles and fortunes of Montreal's three major sports franchises have revolved in the 1990s. Along with the Expos' uncertain future, the once mighty Canadiens are a mediocre hockey team at best these days. In the meantime, the once unpopular football team, the Alouettes, are now filling the seats at downtown McGill Stadium.

Although Canada did very well in both the Olympics and the Pan-Am games, there were new drug controversies along with internal problems within the IOC itself.

Athletes' salaries in all sports continued to go through the roof, along with unheard-of endorsements fees. However, cities throughout Canada were finding it financially difficult to support their teams.

Saddest of all in 1999 was when number 99 – classy Wayne Gretzky – retired from the game of hockey.

ON THE OTHER HAND, WHO AMONGST US WOULD EVEN ATTEMPT THIS SORT OF THING WITHOUT FIRST GETTING AS STONED AS POSSIBLE ON WHATEVER SUBSTANCE WAS HANDILY AVAILABLE?

At the Olympics, traces of marijuana are found in Canadian skier Ross Rebagliati's urine sample.

The Canadian women's curling team shines at the Olympics.

Some IOC members are accused of gaining financial favours.

MEANWHILE, IN EUROPE...

"BRIT" SOCCER FAN...

"SERB"

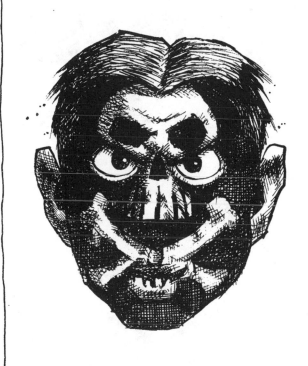

Unruly English fans riot during World Cup while Serbia continues apace.

Expo president Claude Brochu seems intent on selling the team to another city.

Montreal Expo spring training sketchbook, Jupiter, Florida.

BATTING PRACTICE IS WHERE THE REALLY IMPORTANT STUFF GETS TALKED ABOUT...

MANAGER FELIPE ALOU LUNCHES ON CHICKEN SOUP IN HIS OFFICE. PUBLICLY, HIS ONLY CONCERN IS WHAT HAPPENS ON THE FIELD. STILL, YOU HAVE TO WONDER WHAT HE'S THINKING PRIVATELY...

BROADCASTERS JACQUES DOUCET AND RODGER BRULOTTE HORSING AROUND

Remarks by Don Cherry considered insulting to Quebec.

Les Canadiens stink.

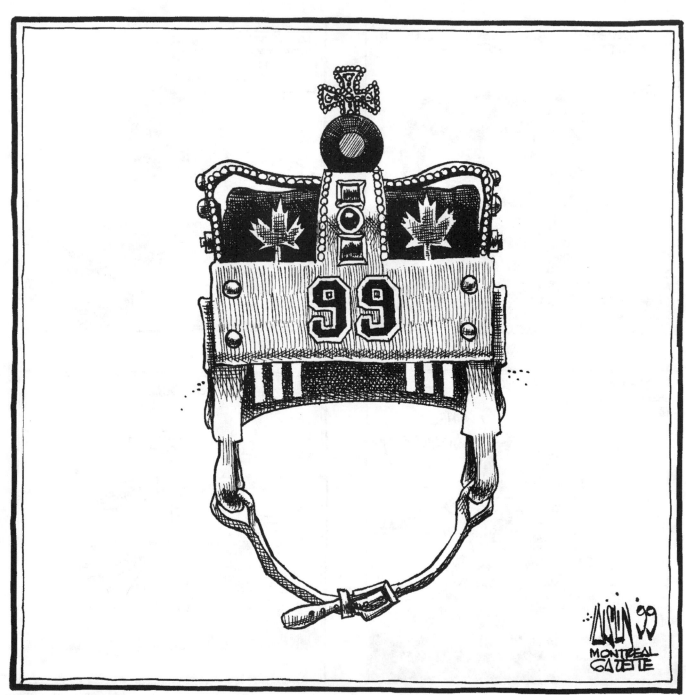

Wayne Gretzky retires.

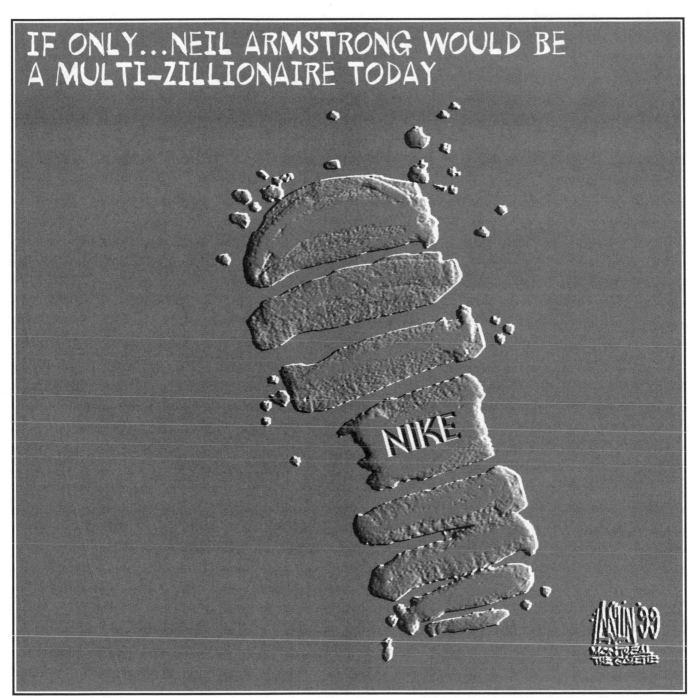

Thirtieth anniversary of the walk on the moon.

Item #1: Popular astronaut Julie Payette flies in space. Item #2: Ronald Corey quits as Canadiens' president.

BiLL CLINTON AND THE REST OF THE WORLD

"Television is democracy at its ugliest."
Paddy Chayefsky

In the late 1990s, the U.S. has enjoyed an unprecedented economic upswing, never mind becoming the world's only remaining superpower. And yet, we seemed to be mostly fascinated with President Bill Clinton's sex life and Monicagate. For Americans this was mere titillation, as it had virtually no effect on the president's popularity in the polls.

Nevertheless, Clinton tried to deflect media attention with several military skirmishes. He whacked Iraq (again), and then got serious by declaring a moral war on the regime of Slobodan Milosevic and Serbia, albeit through NATO.

On the domestic front, America suffered through several terrible mass shootings, seemingly unable to understand that guns (especially in the hands of disturbed individuals) kill people.

Elsewhere, over the last two years, there was the death of Diana, exploding of H-bombs by India and Pakistan, Yeltsin's Russia and little progress towards peace in the Middle East.

THE STATE
of the
UNION...

AISLIN 98
MONTREAL
GAZETTE

116

Captured whale Willie may be set free in ocean.

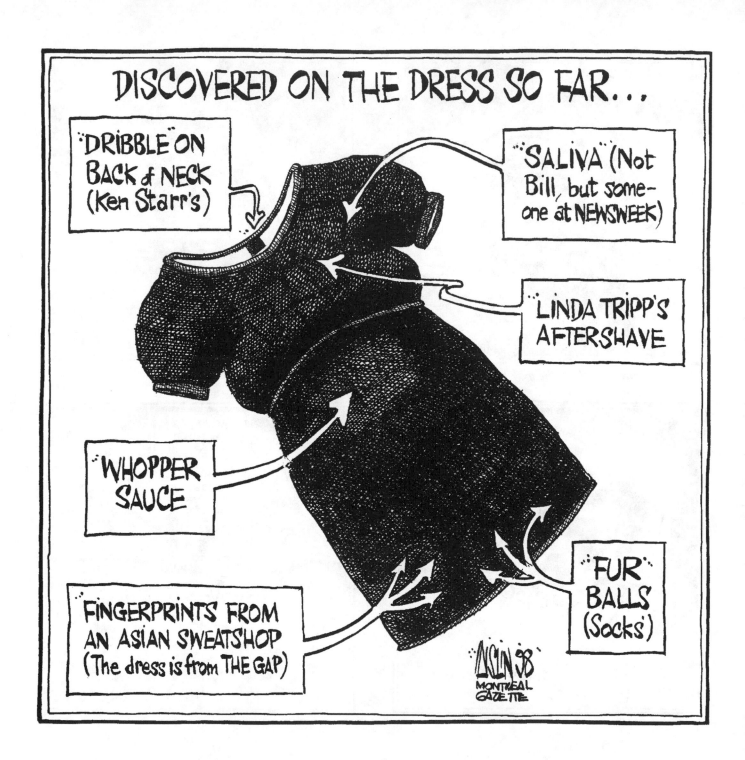

CLOSURE

MILOSEVIC...

AISLIN 98
..MONTREAL GAZETTE

Shooting at Columbine High School in Colorado.

Baghdad bombed at the height of Monicagate.

Mounting tension over Kosovo.

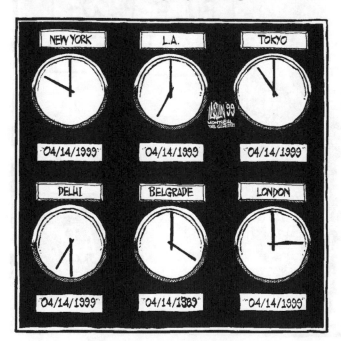

Americans mistakenly bomb Chinese embassy in Belgrade.

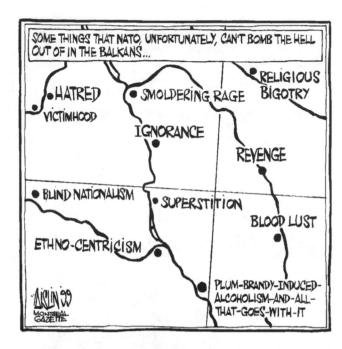

Russian troops invite themselves in as peace keepers.

Canadian forces are part of NATO's peace keeping team in the Balkans.

Will the tabloids back off after the death of Diana?

THIS CORNER **LIKES** THIS IDEA OF UPDATING THE QUEEN'S IMAGE!

The Royal Family is also criticized over its standoffishness after the death of Diana.

India and Pakistan commence the testing of nuclear bombs.

Boris dismisses yet another Prime Minister.

FORMERLY KNOWN AS 1,000 RUBLES, NOW CALLED ONE RUBLE...

FORMERLY KNOWN AS ONE RUBLE, NOW CALLED HALF A RUBLE...

FORMERLY KNOWN AS HALF A RUBLE, NOW CALLED 1/16th OF A RUBLE...

FORMERLY KNOWN AS 1/16th OF A RUBLE, NOW CALLED...

...RUSSIAN WALLPAPER

Financial crisis and inflation in Russia.

Margaret Thatcher once said that the two biggest dangers of the 21st century would be Islamic extremism and the Internet.

The cartoon shown to the right caused more reaction than any I have ever drawn, even if most of it was manufactured by a lobby group in Washington, D.C.

In November of 1997, a radical outfit calling itself the Islamic Group carried out the systematic torture and massacre of 60 harmless tourists in Luxor, Egypt.

This is the most cowardly kind of act, and the horrible death of one small girl angered me in particular. Subsequently, I drew this cartoon of a clearly labelled Islamic extremist as a raving dog (understanding that this is considered an extreme insult in the Arab world, but not in ours – thus the apology to dogs).

The cartoon most certainly was not intended as an attack on the religion of Islam itself.

Our new editorial page editor at The Gazette, Peter Hadekel, flinched, but chose to print the cartoon anyway.

There was no immediate reaction to the cartoon, most Gazette readers sharing my revulsion over the massacre.

However, an outfit in Washington, D.C., named The Council on American-Islamic Relations (CAIR) whose job is to monitor the portrayal of the Arab world closely in the North American Press, began a concentrated campaign against The Gazette and myself demanding an apology several days after the cartoon appeared.

Hadekel began receiving a ton of e-mail from around the world. One petition came from several hundred people of Arab descent in Fort Wayne, Indiana (where, of course, The Gazette is read closely every morning I'm certain).

A demonstration was held in front of The Gazette replete with the burning of copies of the offending cartoon.

The Gazette and Hadekel responded as best they could, by offering closer and more harmonious ties with Montreal's Arab communities.

CAIR, it should be noted, is very hesitant in its denunciation of these massacres when they take place.

The only response a cartoonist can make to this sort of thing is to draw another cartoon, which is on the following page.

The Gazette chose not to publish it.

Sixty innocent tourists are slaughtered by terrorists in Luxor, Egypt.

The Gazette chose not to publish this after the furor over the previous cartoon.

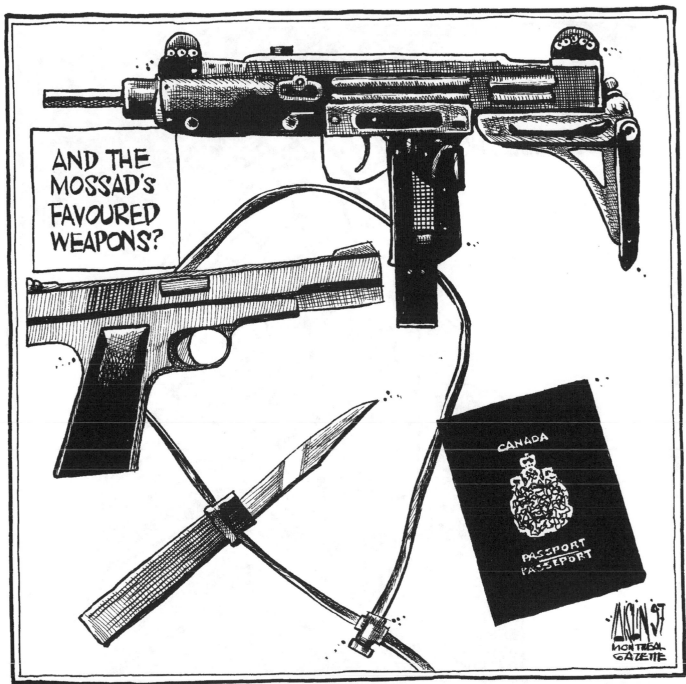

AND THE MOSSAD'S FAVOURED WEAPONS?

Israel's secret police prefer using forged Canadian passports.

137

Mossad hitmen go after Hamas leader.

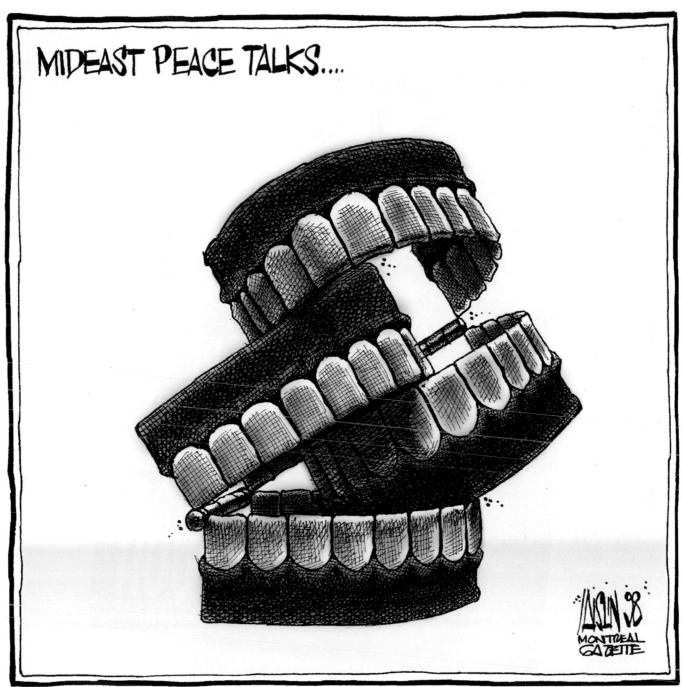

MIDEAST PEACE TALKS....

Grinding on, and on, and on, and on...

In freak trading, the stock market dives for a day.

Book cover for "2000 Reasons to Hate The Millennium", Doubleday, Canada.

YOU AND the FUTURE

"ANNOUNCING THE BANKS' MILLENNIUM PROJECT FOR THE Y2K—INSTALLING VLTs INTO THEIR ATMs!

IDIOT! IDIOT! IDIOT!

PLAY! | Deduct from account | Loan from account

Here on the cusp of the millennium, technology and business rule our lives to a greater degree with every passing minute. Will all these mergers and globalization eventually lead to one currency? ...One big bank? ...One huge company?

Business is sexy again with the rich getting richer and... well, you know. With all governments keen on eliminating deficits and debt (at the behest of big business), there have been cuts in Medicare and other essential services. Unquestionably, we are a less socially - responsible society than we once were. Expect a lot more of the same.

As the Nasty '90s come to an end, we'll be celebrating the millennium with entrepreneurs cashing in on all the hoopla.

Business and technology do like to allow us our toys. We're addicted to our computers, e-mail, the internet, television and, of course, sex (although surveys indicate the interest is more with other peoples' sex lives rather than our own).

And what does Canada have to look forward to in the new millennium? Another Quebec Referendum?

Stay tuned...

HAVE YOU NOTICED HOW COMPANIES ARE GETTING BIGGER?
AISLIN 98
MONTREAL GAZETTE
Universal STUFF Incorporated
...AND COUNTRIES ARE GETTING SMALLER?
BANTAMIA
SNAP
WEELAND
YOURANIA
UPPERSTAN
POP TART
THEIRANIA
CRACKLE
WEEWEELAND
PIDDLE
MYANIA
PUDDLE
LOWERSTAN
GUMBOSTEW
NORTH WHIZ
POP
QUART
WESTALUSIA
EASTALUSIA
VEGGIESTEW
WEST WHIZ
EAST WHIZ
OZ
SOUTH WHIZ
SOUTH EAST WHIZ
S.S.E. WHIZ
PINT
MUTTONLAND
NAVEL
SO, LET'S NOT KID OURSELVES ABOUT WHO ACTUALLY RUNS THINGS!

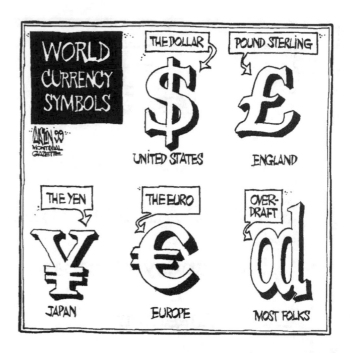

Bell shifts much of its answering system to Arizona.

 ROYAL BANK OF CANADA

Bank of Montreal

BEFORE THE LAYOFFS BEGIN, OUR BIG NEW BANK WILL BE NEEDING A NIFTY CORPORATE LOGO. SO, WHY NOT TAKE THE "ROB" FROM THE ROYAL BANK AND THE "EM" FROM THE BANK OF MONTREAL, AND...?

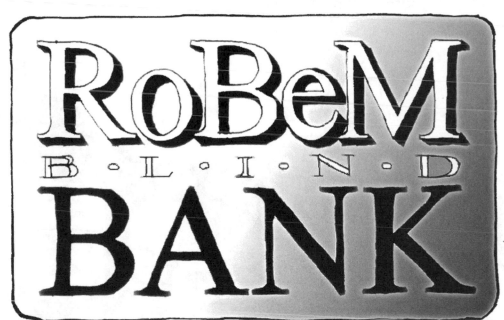

Possible bank merger?

Constant power failures throughout Quebec.

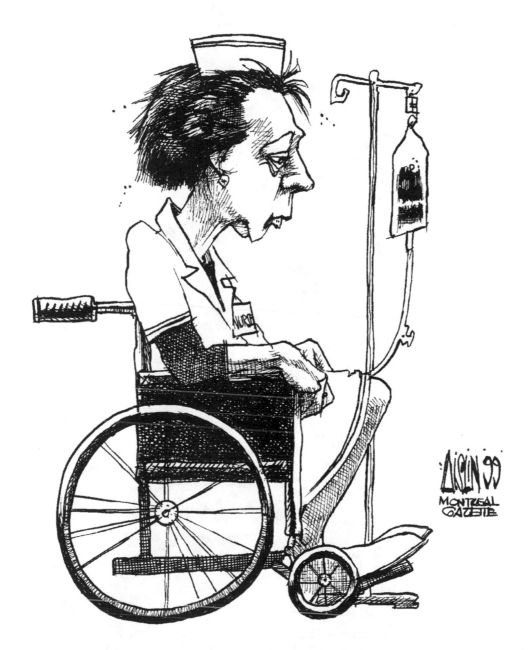

Nurses object to working conditions throughout Canada.

Premier says no to overworked and underpaid nurses.

May West company bought by Montreal company, Saputo Cheese.

Controversial Howard Stern picked up by Toronto and Montreal radio stations.

Court judgement in favour of equality of gay couples.

Stuff, stuff, stuff...

Should we expect the Disneyfying of everything?

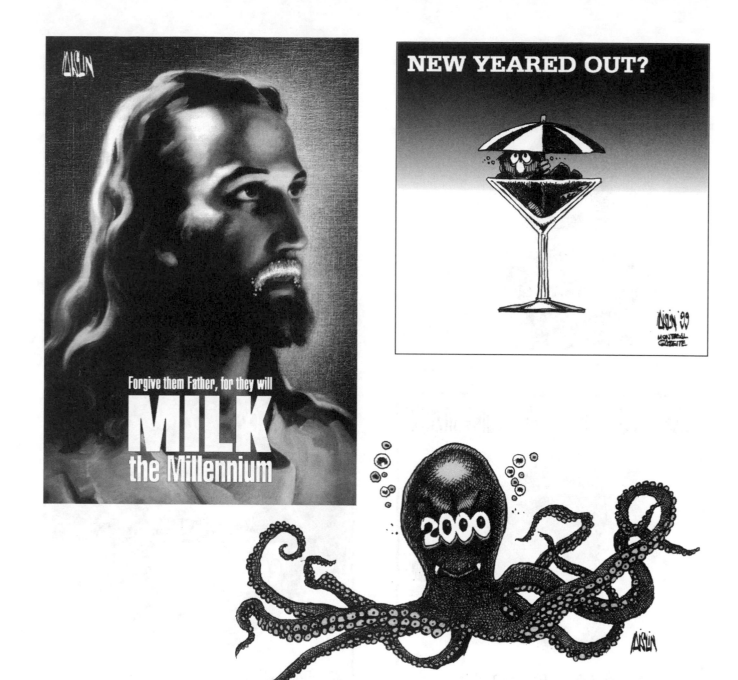

Cartoons from the book "2000 Reasons to Hate The Millennium", Doubleday, Canada.

And, in the new Millennium, yet another Referendum?

AISLIN is the name of Terry Mosher's elder daughter, and the nom de plume he uses as the editorial page cartoonist for The Montreal Gazette. Considered Canada's "nastiest cartoonist," he is syndicated to newspapers throughout Canada. Mosher has freelanced in the U.S. and abroad for such publications as The New York Times, Time Magazine, The National Lampoon, Harper's, The Atlantic Monthly and Punch.

Aislin has travelled extensively on assignment for The Gazette, writing and drawing interpretive sketchbooks throughout Canada, The U.S., Northern Ireland, Russia, Cuba and North Africa.

THE BIG WIND-UP! is Aislin's 30th book. Amongst the others, he co-wrote a book with Peter Desbarats entitled THE HECKLERS, a history of political cartooning in Canada.

An avid baseball fan, Mosher is a twenty-two year member of The Baseball Writers' Association of America, which allows him to vote for Baseball's Hall of Fame in Cooperstown, N.Y.

Montreal's McCord Museum recently hosted a large exhibit of the best caricatures of Aislin of The Gazette and Serge Chapleau, the editorial page cartoonist for La Presse. The exhibition ran for 17 months and attracted 115,000 visitors.

More information, and Aislin's daily cartoon, may be found at: www.aislin.com
Terry Mosher's e-mail address is: aislin@globale.net

Other recent Aislin books available from McArthur & Company.

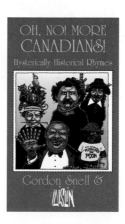